COLLECTED WORKS OF
C. W. VALENTINE

Volume 4

PSYCHOLOGY AND MENTAL HEALTH

PSYCHOLOGY AND MENTAL HEALTH

C. W. VALENTINE

Routledge
Taylor & Francis Group
LONDON AND NEW YORK

First published in 1948

This edition first published in 2015
by Routledge
27 Church Road, Hove BN3 2FA

and by Routledge
711 Third Avenue, New York, NY 10017

Routledge is an imprint of the Taylor & Francis Group, an informa business

British Library Cataloguing in Publication Data
A catalogue record for this book is available from the British Library

ISBN: 978-1-138-89931-5 (Set)
ISBN: 978-1-315-69276-0 (Set) (ebk)
ISBN: 978-1-138-89963-6 (Volume 4) (hbk)
ISBN: 978-1-315-70772-3 (Volume 4) (ebk)

Publisher's Note
The publisher has gone to great lengths to ensure the quality of this reprint but points out that some imperfections in the original copies may be apparent.

Disclaimer
The publisher has made every effort to trace copyright holders and would welcome correspondence from those they have been unable to trace.

PSYCHOLOGY AND MENTAL HEALTH

by

C. W. VALENTINE
M.A., D.PHIL.
Emeritus Professor in the University of Birmingham

METHUEN & CO. LTD. LONDON
36 Essex Street, Strand, W.C.2

First published in 1948

CATALOGUE NO. 3690/U

PRINTED IN GREAT BRITAIN

PREFACE

The chapters of this book are based on five broadcast talks given in the Autumn of 1946. A number of correspondents and others expressed a wish to read the talks, and they are printed largely as given, with some modifications to suit the written word. A concluding chapter and some new paragraphs and footnotes have been added, and part of the first talk has been expanded into a brief introductory chapter.

C.W.V.

The University of Birmingham
March, 1947

CONTENTS

CHAPTER I

INTRODUCTION

Misunderstandings as to psychology. Psychology has been much to the fore of late and misunderstandings about it are frequent and sometimes amazing. It is often confused with psycho-analysis or even with psychical research. Many imagine that Freud was the first psychologist, and that it is "all sex." Misunderstandings as to Freud's views and the extravagant theories of some of his followers have also led to strong antagonism to psychology in some circles including some medical circles.

The misleading statement that "psychologists say" that even the naughtiest children should not be punished has led some experienced teachers and some wise parents, not unnaturally, to the view that "these psychologists" talk a lot of nonsense—as indeed some so labelled do.

Unfortunately it is often difficult for the general public to decide a speaker's or writer's qualifications to deal with psychological questions. Indeed, it is possible at present for anyone with no adequate training in psychology to call himself a psychologist and even advertise himself as a "consulting psychologist," with danger of harm to individuals and to the detriment of the reputation of psychology itself.

The bearing of psychology on problems of mental health has not escaped from these misunderstandings and prejudices. On the one hand extravagant claims for the miracles that psychology can work, independently of any consideration for physical well-being, are opposed by extremists who will have none of it. Others with more reason urge that psychological problems are questions for the expert and no one else should concern themselves with them. If it is meant that psychological treatment should be left to the expert, we may readily agree, but the time for a "hush-hush" policy has passed, if it were ever the right one. If critical and cautious expositions are not given by those who have made a serious study of the subject, the general public will in any case be served with pamphlets and articles of a popular but possibly misleading type, and wrong ideas be spread further abroad.

Such are the reasons which seem to justify the broadcasting of the kind of talks on which these chapters were based, and the publication of the book itself. But there is a further reason. The talks were not concerned merely with those clearly suffering from some neurotic symptom and with the possibility of psychological treatment helping them ; they were also addressed to those larger numbers who, though they carry on their work efficiently and may seem happy enough to their fellows, are nevertheless fighting conflicts within themselves and finding life hard and perhaps lonely ; and to those extra-sensitive folk who feel deeply the attitude of others. I spoke and write for the " tender minded " rather than the " tough minded," to quote William James's famous labels. The tougher type are perhaps usually the happier, but they are no more useful to society as a whole, than are the others.*

The meaning of " mental health " and " mental disorders." Before dealing with our specific topics it may be well to say something as to the meaning of " mental-health " and as to the frequency of minor " mental disorders " First we must get rid of the idea implied in the common use of the term " mental " as meaning either mad or defective in intelligence. Also we must not imagine that we can divide people into two sharply separable

* No doubt there are a good many of the Mrs. Gummidge type who openly proclaim that other people do not " feel things " like they do. But there are also those who do feel deeply and say little or nothing about it. We shall return to this topic in the Chapter on Emotions.

classes—(*a*) the insane and (*b*) those who are perfectly sound in mental health. The ideally healthy mind, or "normal" mind as it is sometimes called, is indeed hard to describe; and the precise margin between normal and abnormal is almost impossible to indicate. But it will be agreed, I think, that we are most of us very unreasonable at times: some are excessively irritated over trivial things; some have violent prejudices against innocent people, others are absurdly devoted to and dominated by a person quite unworthy of their devotion. Some are haunted by ridiculous fears they cannot overcome; some may be profoundly depressed and not know what about; others get mentally tired with very little work, and so on.

All these are kinds of mental ill-health. That does not mean that such people are making for the asylum, though unfortunately in the Army men often referred to the medical psychologist as "the loony doctor." As a matter of fact if we take the symtoms I have just mentioned, most of us at times fall short of perfect mental health, however fit our bodies may be.

The frequency of minor mental disorders or neuroses. We have indeed, some estimates as to the frequency of minor mental disorders or neurotic symptoms. Thus, one medical man reports that of one-thousand insured workers who consulted the doctor about physical ill-health, about one third were found to be suffering from some form of mental disorder.*

Another investigation was carried out among workers in their offices or factories, etc., and not merely on those who were consulting a doctor for physical reasons.

A psychologist and a medical psychologist working together, examined one-thousand people of various types—students as well as workers in factories and offices. It should be noticed that these persons were not referred to them specially; they were a fair average sample of the working population.

The investigators came to the conclusion that nearly two in three showed some signs of mental ill-health or some neurotic symptom, for example, irrational fears or anxiety, obsessive thoughts and actions, etc. One in six was thought bad enough to need treatment or at least to justify further investigation.† The great majority were no doubt carrying on without any serious effect on their work but only on their own happiness, though of this we cannot be certain.

* Report by Dr. J. L. Halliday, quoted by Max Minde *In Search of Happiness* (London, 1937) page 150.

† See the *Nervous Temperament* by Millais Culpin and May Smith (Industrial Health Research Board, Report No. 61. London 1930).

If the figures are at all representative of the general population it means that in businesses and factories (or even in schools or Universities) among a hundred workers there are probably a dozen or more suffering from some minor neurosis that affects their own work or their relationship with others. It means too that in a considerable proportion of marriages the chances are in favour of at least one partner (and in a smaller proportion of cases, both partners) having at least some slight neurotic trouble. Some of these will be unimportant; some slight obsessions for example, may be quite harmless; but in other cases even a minor mental disorder may cause serious trouble, especially if not understood by the other partner. In some cases two neurotic traits—one in each partner—may clash badly.*

The important practical question is as to the *degree* of any irrational feelings or other neurotic symptoms, or the extent to which they interfere with efficient working and co-operative living with others, or with the peace and happiness of the individual.

In the following chapters we shall discuss

* As unhappiness in marriage may itself be a cause of neurosis it will be seen how intimately problems of mental health are linked with those of marital happiness. On this point see Professor L. M. Terman's *Psychological Factors in Marital Happiness*, page 32 and elsewhere.

various causes of some of these minor mental disorders, and some of the ways in which they can be dealt with. We shall include among these some types of mental problems and difficulties which can sometimes be faced and overcome by the individual himself, without psychological treatment.

CHAPTER II

WORK, WORRY AND CONFLICT

Work and "nervous breakdowns." If the mental disorders just described develop too far there is apt to be what is called in popular language a "nervous breakdown." This is often ascribed to "overwork." Now that sounds very praiseworthy ; we all like to think we have been so devoted to work that we have overdone it. Unfortunately the evidence is all against mere work being the cause of mental breakdown. Indeed, experiments have made it doubtful whether there is such a thing as truly *mental* fatigue brought about by mental work ; boredom is often mistaken for fatigue.

One leading authority reports that in five hundred cases of apparent nervous breakdown, only two per cent could be traced directly to overwork.*

During the war years many people worked hard for seven days a week, and though wearied and depressed by many things, were certainly not near a breakdown. Some of us, fortunate

* Henderson and Gillespie, in their standard work *A Text-book of Psychiatry* (pages 64 and 65) suggest that the person suffering from anxiety tends to overwork, and later attributes his morbid anxiety to the overwork.

enough to have really congenial work, were as fit as when we took regular holidays.

Of course excessive hours of work may involve other things. They may mean cutting short sleep, or neglect of fresh air and exercise, or not allowing proper time for meals—sometimes all three ; and unless a man has an iron constitution these are likely in time to mean *physical* disorders and loss of efficiency in work. Also no one questions the possibility of serious effects of great physical fatigue through prolonged overwork.

The strain of emotional conflict. But there is another more serious cause of breakdown when work is excessive, especially where the work involves responsibilities and much dealing with other people. An increase of such work brings with it an increase of problems for solution : of conflict with difficult and irritating people, and often conflict within the self in deciding how to act.

Now one thing psychologists are agreed on is that emotional conflict does exhaust energy. In fact they confirm the old saying that " it's worry that kills, not work."

There are, of course, many sources of inward conflict besides those found in work. Perhaps the most severe of all is that of the brave soldier in the face of grave danger—the conflict between intense fear and the primitive instinct to escape on the one hand and the claims of duty or devotion to his comrades on the other. This has been a cause of breakdown in some devoted soldiers, and the most conscientious are sometimes most liable to it.

Another source of conflict is that due to one of the strong inborn impulses and their accompanying emotions, of sex and passionate love, of pugnacity and anger, of self-assertion and pride ; these are apt to conflict with moral or religious ideals or with social conventions. I shall discuss these conflicts in later chapters.

Even in the more humdrum affairs of everyday life and work, emotional conflicts may arise. The employee who has to curb his anger when bullied by a hard master or, perhaps, more likely nowadays, the employer who has to curb his anger at the laziness or incompetence of some employee for fear of losing him, these may be subject to constant emotional conflict ; never perhaps very intense, but constantly recurring and so the more wearing. Or again it may be working with irritating colleagues, or living with very touchy people who have to be always considered lest they should get huffy. This is especially hard when a house or rooms have to be shared with them, as so often in these days. Constantly having to exercise tact is a mentally fatiguing thing, because of the lurking impulse in us to use other methods. And so people get worried and irritable and too often put it all down to overwork. Physical fatigue make it harder to bear, of course, but even without that, constant emotional conflict is exhausting.

"War strain" and pre-war experiences. Another favourite explanation of nervous upset and fatigue is "War-strain." Of course, if the war brought us grave anxieties as it did to most people, the conflict of fear and hope, or the loss of those dearest, or the ruin of business, or loss of home, then the effects of emotional conflict or strain may follow. But is it not apparent that some who have passed through these most terrible experiences remain calm and placid, kindly and considerate to others, and go on with their daily work in a courageous and noble way? How is this? There are several possible explanations. First they may be favoured with a well balanced temperament, a nervous system which is more stable than the average. Others may have resolved their conflicts on a higher level; perhaps in the consolation of religion they may see their troubles in a new light.

But there is often something further, and I may best explain it by referring to some typical nervous breakdowns of soldiers during the war. In many such cases it was found that the man had been suffering from some severe mental conflict *before* the war—perhaps an unhappy marriage or failure in his work and an inferiority complex and so on. The strain of war proved only " a last straw " (admittedly a rather heavy straw) and often it was found that the mere removal of the war strain did not bring about a cure. For example, one psychologist dealt with a soldier who had lost his memory, and who was extremely feeble physically. He came under the care of the psychologist, Professor McDougall, just after being sent home from the battle-field suffering from extensive loss of memory and general weakness, etc. He had forgotten a great deal about his earlier life and could not even remember whether he was married, though he supposed that a photograph he found in his pocket was one of his wife. McDougall hypnotized him several times and concluded that there was a strong resistance to the recall of memories, especially the recall of experiences in the trenches. Finally McDougall was able to overcome this resistance and the memories were recalled including a detailed description of the horrors witnessed at the front, and eventually of the soldier's home life. An interesting point about this case was that at the recall of the forgotten experiences and the release of the repressions, the patient's physical vigour was greatly increased immediately; he had been tested before for power of hand-grip with a dynamometer and had never been able to force the index beyond the thirty-kilo mark, but within an hour of his recovery of memory he had reached the ninety-kilo mark.*

Sometimes a severe strain in war rouses some earlier mental wound, which remains when the war strain is over. Let me give an illustration of this.

A young soldier came to consult me about the trouble from which he suffered. The gun which he was serving in France was hit by a shell; his sergeant, for whom he had a great affection, was killed, and he himself was temporarily stunned. He recovered from this fairly quickly, sufficiently to get back to active service again, but for some months he suffered from an intense fear of the dark. This was greater when an air-raid warning occurred, but remained also at other times even when there was clearly no danger of an air-raid; so that he was even unwilling to go out with his fiancée after dark or to go to a cinema in

* See the Chapter by W. McDougall in *Functional Nerve Disease* (Edited by Crichton Miller) 1920, page 191. That the war experience, including the so-called "shell-shock," might be only one final cause of breakdown, was emphasized by some psychologists during the first World War. See *Shell-shock and its Lessons*, by G. Elliot Smith and T. H. Pear. (Manchester University Press, 1917).

the evening. By enquiry into his early life I was able to trace two terrifying experiences of his as a boy, which he had almost forgotten, and certainly had never thought of in connection with his present trouble. I cannot give details for fear of the case being recognized but both experiences occurred in the dark, and the second was not only terrifying but involved great emotional conflict. Through our talking over these experiences and my pointing out their probable effect on his attitude towards the dark, considerable relief appeared after two or three visits; he was then quite ready to go out in the dark, and when an air-raid warning sounded, he no longer had the previous intense physical discomfort—his "stomach turning over" as he put it.

That is only one example of many in which psychologists have found that a nervous trouble apparently caused merely by some war experience, did not disappear until earlier troubles were brought to light.

Social strains in work and in the home. Similar phenomena appear in civilian life. Some who have been bombed out of their homes, or have lost those dearest to them, have carried on steadily and well. Others whose extra war-strain has been relatively slight, have become increasingly irritable or shown hysterical crying or lessened control of emotions, or have become excessively depressed. Why is this?

The most reasonable explanation seems to be that before the war such persons were already only just managing to carry on their work placidly and efficiently. Self-restraint in some cases was only maintained with great difficulty, and energy was being exhausted by some hidden conflict, or unconscious repression. The extra strain gives the final blow. The balance is disturbed, and the emotional harmony (secured before only by considerable exhaustion of energy through repression) is now lost.

In many cases it may be easy to discover the sources of trouble. Perhaps a professional worker has been in a state of anxiety about his money affairs for some years, but has kept heart. Now, even though the war does not directly affect his particular work or prospects, the new anxiety added to the old proves too much and he goes under. But in many cases the person does not know what is the real cause of the trouble. We have to investigate the past, and get to *unconscious* influences and buried complexes. These I shall discuss in later chapters. But it would be wrong to suggest that *nothing* can be done about worries and conflicts without the psychologist's help in exploring the unconscious.

In the first place let us take the worry and strain which comes from feeling you are in the wrong job, as many really are. It may be too difficult for a man—involving responsibility which he cannot shoulder ; or it may be too simple and mechanical for his good abilities. Some people hate routine and monotony in work though some actually prefer it.

Now I know there are many lazy people who are never contented with their job ; they are constantly wanting to move on to another, and the fault is never with them, of course. We need have little sympathy with them ; but I am concerned here about the hard working conscientious person, with a sense of responsibility and worried about the future. For the middle-aged and older, it is no doubt usually too late to change : but for the younger it is worth while giving some serious study to the question of the kind of work they are really fitted for. If their sole idea is to make the most money they can, and they do not care about the kind of work, then this is not their problem. But many people would be happier if they were in the kind of work they can do best and like, rather than in other kinds with better pay.

There are other sources of worry and waste of nervous energy in connection with work or home. Sometimes in a factory a worker and a foreman cannot get on together, whereas the worker may get on quite well under a different foreman if the change can be made. Frequently in an office two people just cannot " hit it off " though each gets on well with others. In the Army it sometimes happened that a man could carry on well while under one officer, but broke down under another. An interesting case is described by J. E. W. Wallin* of a teacher who was keen on his work but thought he had an inferiority complex. Under one Head Teacher, however, he did well and kept his class a year. He was then moved to another school where the Principal was austere and self-important. The effect was such that the teacher had a " nervous breakdown."

Matters may be similar in home relationships. Often they can be adjusted but sometimes this seems impossible. The French psychologist Janet† tells of one case in which a mother and grown daughter lived alone together and " got on one another's nerves." They were advised to live apart but near to one another, and they then got on much better and were much more fond of one another.

The coventional idea that a near relative

* In his book *Minor Mental Maladjustments in Normal People* (Duke University Press 1939) page 215.

† In his fascinating book *Psychological Healing*, (2 Volumes).

ought to see a lot of another just because he is a relative, is often carried too far.

Sometimes, in these conflicts and incompatabilities between fellow-workers or individuals in the home, unconscious forces are at work. They may be fundamental and influence the whole relationship. Sometimes they may be due to neurotic symptoms which may eventually be cured; sometimes the unconscious causes may be very specific and reveal themselves in rather petty cases of irritability. For example, one man got excessively angry when his wife fidgeted with a carving knife at table, until it was found that when he was a small boy his father had been apt to hit him on the hand at meal times with a carving knife, for slight misdemeanours.

Attitudes to troubles. More serious unconscious causes of conflict I shall refer to in later chapters. But I do not want to appear to suggest that we can never do anything in these conflicts or worries or hardships of every-day life, without psychological help. Sometimes a contented attitude itself, or the resolution to make the best of a bad job, makes a world of difference: witness the usual attitude of the Britisher in war days or of the housewife in difficulties about food and housing, grousing, perhaps, but usually grimly or even cheerfully bearing up. Much depends on our attitude to what we get. My sister once had a charwoman, a wife and mother, who went on with her work year after year without any holiday. "No," she said once, "I ain't never had no holiday—excepting my confinements!" Yes, the way we look at things may even change their appearance.

Again, there is the influence of religion. Now it is not the business of the psychologist to discuss the truth of religion: but whether true or not, there is no gainsaying the fact that it makes a world of difference if a man *can* face his troubles and say with the apostle, "these light afflictions, which are but for a moment, work out a far more exceeding and eternal weight of glory."

Even if we cannot accept the teachings of religion, something can be done by facing the situation squarely; by searching ourselves and seeing whether we are at fault and if we are expecting too much of others and too little of ourselves.

Sometimes, however, in reasonable and even in religious people, there are deep unconscious causes of mental trouble, which cannot be got rid of by just trying hard to live up to an ideal. These buried cancers of the mind have to be dug out. We shall discuss them more fully in the next chapter.

CHAPTER III

REPRESSIONS, IRRITABILITY AND COMPLEXES

In the last chapter we saw that hard work was rarely the cause of nervous breakdown or mental disorder, but rather worry and emotional conflict. We saw that sometimes we can deal with the causes of such conflict or worry by conscious control, and by getting rid of the causes if we know them. But often we do not know the causes; they are buried in the unconscious or as we say "repressed."

Let us consider some examples of repression, first one of an extreme kind, fortunately not common. It is the story of a young woman engaged to be married to a shoe-maker.* At the last moment he jilted her. The emotional shock was so severe that she lost her reason and had to be removed to an asylum. The painful memory of the false lover was completely repressed and forgotten; yet its continued influence was shown in this: all day this poor woman was constantly making movements

* The case is reported by Jung and described by Dr. Bernard Hart in his book *The Psychology of Insanity*, page 115.

with her hands like those of a shoemaker sewing shoes.

Now this example need not cause alarm. It is true that repression is fairly common, and probably most of us have our repressions though we may not know it ; but this was an extreme case, which I gave because it illustrates so well two things : first that a profound emotional experience may be repressed to the extent of complete forgetting. Second, that the repressed experience may express itself in a symbolic form ; the woman made movements like those of a cobbler mending shoes.

Our next examples are of less serious but commoner kinds. Hundreds of reports of the same type have been given by psychologists of different views. For whatever differences there may be among psychologists (and let us recall the warning given in Chapter I that some persons call themselves psychologists who have no qualification to do so) whatever differences of views there are on some things, on this all competent psychologists would agree, that severe mental conflict may result in repression and forgetting, and yet the repressed experience may go on affecting our conscious life ; it forms what we call a " complex " : something buried in the unconscious.

For example, a young man once consulted

me about a terrible feeling of fear which often came over him. He was not afraid of any particular thing; he just felt a dreadful emotion of fear. I put him through various kinds of psychological tests. As the result of these there was brought back to his mind the memory of intense fear he had experienced as a boy when troubled about certain sex developments of which he had been left in entire ignorance. We now discovered that the circumstances which had recently caused the mysterious paroxysms of fear, had certain connections with the fears of boyhood and with their causes. This explanation gave him immense relief, and made possible a new attitude towards situations which had tended to revive them, so that the fears never recurred again.*

Repressions and complexes are sometimes very serious and sometimes rather trivial. Let me give an amusing example of a less serious type. Some years ago I was lecturing to a large psychology club. I talked about the way forgotten experiences of childhood may affect us in later life. In the discussion

* By the way I have come across a number of cases in which ignorance about simple facts of sex development or a wrong attitude to sex have caused great trouble to young people later on. A case in which a marriage was being ruined by such a wrong attitude is described in Chapter VI.

that followed, a man in the audience said that I had made him wonder about a certain eccentricity of his own. He said he could not bear to sit on a public platform, and that the chair next to me was empty because he, the Vice-President of the Society, refused to sit on a platform, although he did not mind addressing that large audience from the floor. Now he had just remembered an early experience. When a small boy at school, he had gone into the girls' cloakroom with several other boys and dressed up in girl's clothes, The Head Master caught him, and him only, and his punishment was that he had to sit all day in the girl's clothes on the platform in the central hall of the school, with the pupils constantly passing and jeering at him. " Now," said the Vice-President to me, " I wonder if you think this was the cause of my hatred of platforms ; and if so, what would you advise me to do ? " I said I thought it probably was the cause and that now he knew he had had a sympathetic and not a jeering audience I would urge him to come up on the platform there and then. (I well remember how a Yorkshireman at the back called out, " Ay, go oop and 'ave a try "). The Vice-President thereupon came to the platform, sat down on the chair, and declared afterwards that he felt none of his old fear or discomfort.

Now one interesting thing about this case was that the man had not entirely forgotten the childish experience: but he had never thought of it as being the cause of his hatred of platforms; there had been "dissociation" rather than complete "repression," and that seems to happen sometimes with what we may call milder complexes. But once the original cause of the eccentricity or nervous trouble is realised, we can often see things in a new light and see how foolish the whole business is.

When is repression harmful? A word should be said about the meaning of this word "repression" and the question as to its harmfulness. I imagine we all know what it is to say to ourselves, "No, I won't let myself do that" or "I won't let myself feel that about so and so," in spite of a strong urge to do so. Now, if this kind of thing is kept clearly conscious, no harm is likely to result. Or suppose there is conflict between two powerful motives, say between the strong appeal of sex and the force of moral ideals or of social convention; or in war, the terrible conflict between fear in the presence of danger and a strong sense of duty. Here again there is general agreement among psychologists that a deliberate calm choice of A rather than B, with full awareness of the sacrifice involved in giving up B, is the healthy attitude. The conflict may still be severe : it may cause pain and exhaust energy : but it is not likely to cause a nervous breakdown or "neurosis."

When is there danger then ? Let me quote a leading authority on this. "Danger of disorder comes when the contending motives work obscurely, unrecognized or disguised by reasons which we invent to explain our yielding to the promptings we do not acknowledge ; and especially is there danger of disorder when one of the unrecognized motives is of such a nature that we will not, dare not, recognize it but rather repress it."*

One example of that would be the prudish spinster who refuses to admit to herself that she could possibly have such a horrid thing as sex feeling ; another example would be the conscientious soldier who is unwilling to recognize that he fears death : though the real hero in battle is not the man who feels no fear, but he who does his duty in spite of it.

Why repression causes a mental disorder and often exhausts energy is a difficult problem to discuss briefly ; but we are faced with the plain fact that when these repressions are released the beneficial effects are often immediate. In some cases a basic instinctive source of energy may be linked up with

* See W. McDougall's, *Outline of Abnormal Psychology*, page 217.

activities from which it has been cut off.*

Irritability. Let us consider another kind of trouble sometimes due to repression and still more common in everyday life. Why does a man sometimes burst out in anger over some little thing that irritates him? The anger seems out of all proportion to the cause, and he may really like or even love the person he gets angry with. Irritability may of course be induced by lack of sleep or through being physically out of sorts. Here I am assuming that physical condition is normal and that nevertheless there are excessive and irrational outbursts of irritability.†

Often these sudden outbursts happen because the man had been repressing many little irritations before, and then there comes again that "last straw"; his mental balance is disturbed and out come all the annoyance

* I have discussed the nature and types of repression in my book *The New Psychology of the Unconscious*. Fuller treatment will be found in McDougall's comprehensive book just quoted.

† The first thing for a non-medical psychologist to do with a patient is to make sure that a recent medical report indicates that the mental disorder cannot have a physical cause, unless of course, the nature of the trouble makes it perfectly clear that it is psychological. Probably in most cases, however, physical conditions play some slight part and it is surprising how often one of the first things a psychologist has to do is to recommend a visit to a medical man.

and anger which have been bottled up. Now we are all likely to find some things irritating—though some placid folk seem able to stand unlimited amounts. When there are conscious sources of irritation between two people it may be well to talk things over quietly: and for one to avoid things which irritate the other even if they seem trivial. It may seem silly to a man that his wife objects to his knocking out his pipe in the empty grate: but if it really irritates her and she much prefers him to use an ash-tray, why not pacify her? If the husband cannot stand a certain kind of hat why not humour him, even if that hat would appeal more to other women?

In some cases the repetition of some action or type of remark by A to which B has frequently shown his objection, may lead to a specially marked outburst which seems out of proportion to the triviality of the action. Such outbursts may be due to A's feeling (conscious or repressed) that B does not care enough for A to note or remember his objection.*

* Professor J. K. Folsom in his comprehensive study *The Family* (page 495) makes the extreme statement that marriage is a lifelong contest between love and irritation (or disgust or fear). If our argument above is sound it will be seen that the relation between love and irritation may be more complex than Folsom's statement might at first seem to make it.

Sometimes irritability seems to result from a repressed feeling of inferiority. An assertive or dominating man may become irritable or lose his temper when you touch on a weak point in his argument which he must see to be weak if he can be brought to face it. But he may be repressing the thought of the weakness of his position, especially if it is connected with a defect in his own character which he will not acknowledge to himself.

Some psychologists hold that when a man represses the idea of some particular weakness in himself, say selfishness or conceit, he tends especially to imagine he can detect it in some other persons (to "project" it on them) and so gets particularly irritated by them.*

A different cause may be at the bottom of irritability which shows itself in a tendency to revolt against certain kinds of restraint or discipline. This may be due to a revival of the antagonism to the father's (or mother's) discipline. That discipline may have been too severe, or it may have been quite reasonable but resented by an exceptionally self-assertive child. Then later in life any person who in some way unconsciously recalls the father and his domination, may arouse the complex, and the result is a violent reaction.

* On this point see J. A. Hadfield, *Psychology and Morals*, page 34 (Methuen 1923).

Sometimes this occurs in quite trivial things. In one case I dealt with, a man became absurdly irritated when teased about his fondness for certain food delicacies. He would become very angry about it and then try to justify it. We began to explore the possibility of the influence of his experiences as a child : and his interest was intense when he recalled that his father, who had been a severe and dominating parent, had frequently criticized him, even when a young man, for wanting these particular delicacies, which the father himself did not happen to like ! After this explanation the teasing was not resented in the slightest, but only caused mild amusement.

The irritability of clever people. It is generally recognized that, in the normal person, anger is caused chiefly by the hindrance of a strong impulse to action or of self-assertion. Now some very clever people seem specially apt to be irritable owing to the constant frustration of their quick working minds by the stupid or indifferent. As the saying goes, they cannot " suffer fools gladly."

An example of this is the teacher who gets irritated by the slowness of the pupil to understand. The puzzle is that even a good teacher may find himself getting exasperated by the stupidity of a pupil though the teacher may know that the pupil is trying his best. The teacher may also know that bad temper is useless and even harmful ; and yet it goes on. Why is this ? It is possible first that he may be one with an excessively strong innate tendency to anger—unfortunate if so because we need teachers of equable temperament. Sometimes, however, this temper may be due primarily to the frustration of a genuine desire to help the pupil : but it is an irrational and foolish outlet, and if the teacher is led to see this and to reflect on its futility, then he is well on the way to checking it : and of course, the same thing applied in other professions and occupations.

To sum up as to irritability : I think we must admit that in many cases (perhaps in most) excessive irritability and bad temper are primarily due to an unusually strong inborn tendency to self-assertion or anger, unchecked by wise training in childhood and youth. Where, however, irritability shows itself only in peculiar situations, or between those who are anxious to help one another, or even between two who love one another, it is well to look for underlying motive forces and even unconscious complexes. One common type of these, the inferiority complex, we shall discuss in the next chapter.

Neurotic symptoms as " defence mechanisms." In closing this chapter I would like to give the warning that bringing to light the unconscious influence, and reviving the repressed memories, impulses, or conflicts, may involve some pain and sacrifice. For often a neurotic symptom is a kind of " defence mechanism " protecting the personality from something which is felt to be intolerable.

In war time for example, it is possible for a most conscientious and brave soldier to develop some trouble which prevents him from going back to the front line ; perhaps his right arm is paralysed. He may be eager to get cured and resume duty, and ready to undergo any treatment advised. It may be found that there are no physical grounds for this paralysis : the patient when hypnotized and told to move his arm may do so easily. But there is an unconscious motive for the paralysis ; it prevents the soldier's return to the fighting front, the fear of which he has been repressing.*

In civilian life we not infrequently come across the same phenomenon. Some illness is developed which safeguards the patient from a burden he finds unbearable.

A good example of such a " defence mechanism " protecting a person from an intolerable

* Examples of this type of " hysterical " symptom as it is labelled will be found in most of the books in the list at the end of this book. See for example *The Neurosis in War*, edited by E. Miller.

task is the following, given by Dr. T. A. Ross.* A woman patient always felt extreme exhaustion when at home; but the exhaustion disappeared whenever she went away. It turned out that at home she had to look after a mother who was suffering from serious mental disorder. When the daughter was led to see that her feeling of exhaustion was really an unconscious defence against a most unpleasant task, her sense of duty enabled her to go back home, do her most difficult job, and yet keep well.

The most striking example of this kind that has come within my own experience is that of a young man who was said to be suffering from deafness after serious air-raids. Two doctors had declared that there was no organic cause of deafness. I found that he could actually hear birds twittering, but could not hear the speech of certain people in his home. He could hear his employer but he could not hear me, though I shouted my loudest. Further psychological and biographical investigations suggested that he was deaf to persons who might broach a certain very painful topic. The giving of this explanation to the patient resulted in an astonishing sudden improvement, so that he could hear me even when I spoke

* In his admirable book *The Common Neuroses*, (2nd edition, London 1937).

very softly ; and on his return home he could also hear the relatives to whom he had been deaf before.

Such a case of psychological deafness is not common ; more frequent examples of unconscious means of defence, against unwelcome duties or unbearable strains, are some of those mysterious aches and pains, often severe and prolonged, but for which the doctor can find no explanation.

Of course in many cases anxiety may directly affect bodily conditions and processes, as we have seen. For example worry about an examination may result in actual physical sickness on the morning of the examination.* But sometimes the change from bodily distress of some kind to physical fitness is too sudden to be so explained.

Bringing back the repressed troubles, the shirked problems or the causes of irritability, may not at first be pleasant ; it may indeed be painful as in some cases just described ; but on this I will quote a fine passage by the psychologist Jung.† First, he says, we do not help the neurotic patient by freeing him from the demands of civilization, but rather by

* See Chapter V (page 54) for some examples of the physical effects of emotions.

† See his *Collected Papers on Analytical Psychology* page 224, (London 1916).

inducing him to face up to the tasks before him. Then he goes on: "The suffering which the patient undergoes in performing this duty takes the place of his neurosis. But whereas the neurosis and the complaints that accompany it are never followed by the delicious feeling of good work well done, of duty fearlessly performed, the suffering that comes from useful work and from victory over real difficulties, brings with it those moments of peace and satisfaction which give the human being the priceless feeling that he has really lived his life."

CHAPTER IV

DEPRESSION, INFERIORITY AND LONELINESS

Reasonable and irrational depression. There are many different kinds of depression and very varied causes of it. Sometimes it is due to poor physical health, even if there is no sign of actual disease. So for a man depressed without any obvious reason, the first thing is to have a thorough examination by a doctor. Even if there is nothing serious it may turn out that there has been neglect of some necessary conditions of bodily health; and if these are attended to, the depression may disappear.*

Again there are many *reasonable* grounds for deep depression: the loss of a dear one, the falseness of someone we have loved deeply, failure in one's main life work and so on. It is quite normal for such things to cause great

* If depression is continuous and profound, so that all interest is lost in life, or if melancholia alternates with periods of elation, the case should be regarded as serious and a psychiatrist consulted. The possibility of suicide in such serious cases must be borne in mind. In this chapter we are concerned with less serious types of depression, though there are all gradations of the trouble.

depression and for these the psychologist as such, has little to say beyond what is usually said by wise friends or by ministers of religion ; but I would stress two things which may afford help to some. First, these sorrowful experiences, if we do not allow them to embitter us, may give us a deeper understanding of others, and a greater power of sympathy which will in time win us more genuine friendship than if we had lived a life of ease and good fortune. Second, depression may sometimes be overcome by the deliberate will to develop new interests and new friendships. But we must be prepared for a period of effort in which we seem to gain no benefit. Only slowly can new interests or activities be built up to take the place of what we have lost.

Often, however, people who have not suffered any of the greater misfortunes of life, are the victims of frequent depression, a depression which seems to others groundless and irrational, *if* they observe it ; but often a man's depression is unknown to those around. Let us consider some of the causes of such depression.

The feeling of inferiority. Sometimes, the depression arises from a feeling of inferiority, of a fear of failure in life. Now this is a much commoner feeling than is supposed : for often it is concealed by an attempt to appear confident, and even by blustering and boasting ;

these are indeed the signs of a true "inferiority complex," when the feeling of inferiority is so painful that it is repressed and no longer conscious.

But just now I am not referring to those suffering from a true inferiority *complex*, but to those who are very conscious of their inadequacy, the humble folk who think too little of themselves. Now they are often quite mistaken. For example, among three hundred University students over half reported that they had suffered from persistent feelings of inferiority in intelligence: yet it is quite certain that University students are well above the average intelligence, though some of their teachers may think otherwise at times.

In some cases this feeling of inferiority may be due to an excessively strong impulse of self-submission—something inborn: and the psychologist can often help a man to realize this. Sometimes this inborn tendency is further increased by specially bad luck in the management of his affairs, by the "slings and arrows of outrageous fortune." One patient of mine complained to me that he was a failure; he could not get on; he had tried this and that and not succeeded. He said he was stupid and lacking in grit, and he was profoundly depressed about it. Now it was possible after a time to show this man that he was far from being stupid, indeed, that he was well above average intelligence: also that his failures had been largely due to circumstances over which he had no control, to pure bad luck on several critical occasions. But I also found that his feeling of inferiority had been first fixed in boyhood by a relative who had brought him up very harshly, constantly telling him what a fool he was. There were some other complications which I need not deal with now: but with these also adjusted the man became more confident and cheerful and tackled some new work with energy.

Even where the person really is inferior in ability and knows it, there is much that can be said by way of comfort. First there is the plain fact that character is as important in life as high intelligence, and that conscientious devotion to work has carried many a man beyond his cleverer but less reliable competitors. Besides, happiness depends as much on our social relations with other people as on our ability to succeed in material things; and everyone, however dull, can, if he tries, be kindly and trustworthy and can win affection. Certainly the man who thinks too little of himself is much more likeable than the one who thinks himself a fine fellow.

The feeling of loneliness. Depression often takes the form especially of a feeling of loneliness. There are some who, without feeling inferior, cannot get on with others and cannot make friends. Some are very sensitive to the smallest criticism ; they expect others always to make a fuss of them, but do little in return. They want to be loved for themselves alone : but they feel that nobody cares for them and they are oppressed with a feeling of loneliness.

Now this is a broad description of various kinds of people, but in many cases this kind of trouble means that the person is suffering from a " mother complex." He or she was excessively petted in childhood and remained too much dependent on the mother through the critical period of adolescence and possibly even in young manhood or young womanhood.

At the time of adolescence the youth should begin to show less dependence on parents, and it is natural for strong friendships to be made with other young people ; but in some cases the excessive devotion of the mother is so pleasant to him that he still clings to her. When teased or criticized by his fellows, he finds it a great comfort to be told what a fine boy he is and to be praised and spoilt at home. (Sometimes it is the father who is concerned but usually it is the mother).

All this may lead in later life to an expectation that others will make a similar fuss about him ; he will resent all criticism and expect others to give, while he makes little return. Naturally he finds very few who will do this ; and then he complains of loneliness and depression and that no one understands him. Indeed, as one leading authority has put it, " When the neurotic complains that the world does not understand him, he is really crying for his mother."

Seeking friends. There are some who are lonely because they are vainly seeking a friend who will be *perfect*—who will understand them completely and appreciate every side of their nature, who will love them for their own sakes, asking nothing in return and even take no interest in anyone else.

If this kind of thing is extreme and the feeling of loneliness is strong and persistent, there is probably a need for a psychological investigation. But for milder types, something may be said on the conscious level. For example, one woman who had sought this ideal of perfection and devotion in a single person, and who was losing her interest in life, made considerable progress when she was led to see that she could distribute her affection among several persons, in such a way as not to expect *everything* from the same person. And similarly we may find that one aspect of our personality is appreciated by one person, another part by one or two others, and so on.

As this woman afterwards put it, " I found it necessary to cut up my heart into little bits : nobody wanted all of it, for it is so exacting and so large. At long last I learned to love people without trying to *absorb* them."*

Sometimes the lonely person cannot make an effort to be friendly ; he always waits for others to make an approach. But clearly if everyone waited for others to make the first friendly approach, none would ever be made ! This is a matter in which sometimes a sympathetic and understanding friend can do much ; but for some it may need the psychologist to help by discovering the cause of such excessive shyness or reserve. In the case of one young man who could not enter a social group without extreme nervousness and diffidence, I had to trace his dependence back, not to parents but to a grandmother who was devoted to him and on whom he had been very dependent. Only then did the weakness and diffidence disappear.

For quite normal persons who are lonely we still need more opportunities for meeting different types of people, in various kinds of societies, clubs and so on. It is like choosing a mate ; you need a wide circle of acquaintances if you are to be sure of finding just those few

* The case is described by Janet in his *Psychological Healing* (Volume II, page 1028).

friends who will suit your temperament and interests and with whom you can become really intimate.

Relief through expression. Whatever the cause of the feeling of loneliness or inferiority and depression, some relief may often be found by merely telling another about it. Some of our great poets, indeed, have said they found relief from deep sorrow by expressing it in verse. For example, Tennyson, mourning for his lost friend, Hallam, wrote :

"I sometimes feel it half a sin
To put in words the grief I feel,
For words, like nature, half reveal
And half conceal the soul within.
But for the unquiet heart and brain
A use in measured language lies :
The sad mechanic exercise
Like dull narcotics, numbing pain."

And Wordsworth wrote :

"To me alone there came a thought of grief ;
A timely utterance gave that thought relief,
And I again am strong."

Few of us could put our feelings into poetry, and if we tried to do so we might find our own verse more depressing than what we are trying to get rid of ! But happy is the man who has so intimate and trustworthy a friend that he can open his full heart to him. For worries and feelings of depression and loneliness may take on a lighter appearance in the mere putting them into words for another, and still more through sympathy and understanding.

Sometimes, however, a man feels that his depressions are too foolish to tell to a friend, or too groundless, or perhaps the grounds are unworthy, or wrong. Here is where the psychologist may help ; not only to seek out the cause but to provide one whose business it is, not to blame or praise, but simply to discuss : so that a man can tell things which he would be ashamed to tell a friend, and even things which he knows to be wrong.

Also a trouble is often made worse because a man thinks it very rare and peculiar, and the mere assurance that many others have felt the same sometimes brings astonishing relief. This is especially the case with adolescents.

In some more serious cases, the patient after a time feels he must repeat again the story of his troubles and receive again the psychologist's guidance and help in the new adjustments that have to be made. New ideas and new attitudes cannot always be adopted immediately. Janet, indeed, tells of one woman who felt she simply had to come to him about every six months and tell him the same old trouble and get his reassurances repeated : and then she would go away happy and satisfied for another six months.

The craving for understanding. Lastly the feeling of loneliness may depend chiefly on the idea that no one understands us. Of course, no one understands anyone else completely; but the neurotic sometimes has an excessive craving for being "understood." He craves for understanding because he feels that only one who understands him can and will truly sympathize. The difficulty is, of course, that such cravings for understanding and sympathy *may* be just the signs of a very self-centred person; or they may be the signs of genuine need in one who is not understood by those around. For as we shall see in the next chapter, the outward expression of a man's feelings and emotions are often misleading to others, and the motives for his actions may be quite misunderstood. But an abnormal craving for sympathy and understanding is probably a sign of unconscious influences, perhaps of regression to a childish attitude; and here the psychologist can often help by showing that very understanding which the patient has never had before, and by affording a new and real sympathy. And so the sufferer may come to have faith, first in the psychologist and then finally in himself and in the possibility of standing on his own feet and facing his difficulties like a man.

Need we say "like a man"? Let me

conclude this chapter with the words of a woman, that brave young spirit Emily Brontë :

“ Yes, as my swift days near their goal
'Tis all that I implore
In life and death a chainless soul,
With courage, to endure.”

CHAPTER V

EMOTIONS AND HOW THEY AFFECT US

Suppose a man in violent anger and jealousy strikes a wife he dearly loves, and bitterly regrets it afterwards. He is likely to say, "I was not myself." A woman in profound grief at the sudden death of her husband may even kill her child and commit suicide. If she has previously been a devoted mother, the inquest report is likely to be "Suicide while temporarily insane." She was "not herself" we say. These are simple examples of the fact that an emotion may be so intense that it gets complete control of a man and makes him do things quite inconsistent with his normal character.

Some physical effects of emotion. It is a familiar fact that the *bodily* effects of an emotion may be very great. We know how violently the heart may beat when we are frightened, how a man flushes in anger and so on. But more hidden things are going on too. Small but important organs called "glands" are stirred to activity. Experiments have showed that feeding a dog for five minutes produced in twenty minutes the flow of a certain quantity of gastric juice needed for digestion. But if the dog was first infuriated by the presence of a cat, five minutes feeding hardly produced any gastric juice.

Now anger or distress at meal times may have a similar effect on people : and sometimes the consequences may be troublesome. For example, one woman for some years complained of indigestion, and medical treatment failed to cure it. Careful enquiry then revealed that she only met her father at meal times and then he was extremely irritable and there was always a scene. She came to dread meals, and so the digestive process was always checked and she had great discomfort which was thought to be due to an ulcer, wrongly as it proved.* There is no doubt that instead of having a heated argument over supper it is much better to listen to "*Itma*."

Inborn differences in emotionality. Why are some people so bad tempered and others so placid ? Why are some so fearsome and others so calm or even reckless in danger ?

First, there are differences in the *inborn* tendencies to feel emotions and the accompanying impulses. Just as one baby is born healthy and another with some serious bodily defect, just as one is born with normal abilities or

* See R. D. Gillespie *The Mind in Daily Life*. (Methuen 1933).

even with latent genius while others can be recognized as hopeless idiots after a few months, so some are born with a strong tendency to be emotional and others placid, some agressive and ready to be angry, which they show before the age of two, and others gentle and pliable.

These inborn tendencies to emotions are closely connected with impulses to action and with strong emotions a man tends to be *impulsive* in action. But that is putting it too simply. For intelligence and reflection on consequences can control strong emotions before they have developed too far ; and strong emotion, well directed, can be a source of power and influence. One of our leading psychologists, Sir Cyril Burt, told me that when he met Lloyd George he at once got the impression of a man of intense emotions ; and yet he soon saw that Lloyd George's high intelligence had these emotions under control. And were not our hearts stirred within us by Churchill's strong emotion and forceful utterance in his broadcasts during the great crises of the war ? In general, the influence of great leaders and great orators, political or religious, depends on the intensity of their own feelings about the cause they advocate, as well as on the ability with which they present it.

The need for harmonizing impulses. The child starts life as a bundle of impulses and emotions competing and conflicting with one another; assertiveness and submission; tendencies to anger and fear, curiosity and wonder. Later comes tender feeling and protectiveness which he shows to a younger child or his animal pets; later still comes the sex urge and its disturbing emotions.

Now if there is to be a harmonious life and mental peace, these various impulses and emotions must somehow be brought under control, and into something of a unity. Many people seem never to achieve this; they are creatures of the impulse of the moment. Their emotions alternate quickly, perhaps violently, though they may really be shallow.

We see unity and harmony brought about in some men through a dominating aim—ambition or devotion to his family, or by religion. But to remain at the mercy of the emotion and the impulse of the moment is to remain a child. The mature mind should be largely *unified* by some dominating aim or ideal. To be made "whole" really means to be made "healthy."

Often there is trouble because a particular impulse and emotion is excessively strong. It may be constant fear of death or of injury, or of ill-health: it may be agressiveness, love of power and the dominance of pride: it may be that sex impulse is overpowering: even a lovely thing like the protective impulse may be abnormally strong and lead parents to foolish indulgence of a child. They may revel in the tender emotion of the moment, without intelligent thought of the future.

The emotion of fear. Let us consider one emotion that dominates the minds of some—the emotion of fear.

Where there is a real object of conscious fear, say of ill-health or business failure, it is well to bear in mind that things are often worse in imagination than they are in reality. To know the worst is often to find that it is not so terrible as we imagined. Sometimes that is because there is now something we can do about it. We can act, and action relieves emotion. Some big game hunters have reported that when beneath the lion's paw or in similar danger they have not felt any fear, their minds were so fully occupied in doing or planning something ; and many a woman, when serious illness has come to one she loved, has found great relief in doing things for the loved one.

Intense *grief*, too, can often be relieved by activity. We may recall how Tennyson in his poem, " Locksley Hall," described the young man who is overwhelmed with grief when jilted by his lover, as saying, " I myself must mix with action lest I wither by despair." That wise man Dr. Johnson was often afflicted with melancholy. When asked how a man should fight melancholy, he said it was madness to try to *think* it down ; rather a man should seek congenial company, read interesting books, keep active, and in fact divert himself by any means he said, except by taking to drink. (Dr. Johnson's particular weakness of course was *tea*).

But to return to fear. There are other kinds of fear, perhaps a vague anxiety always haunting a man—fear of he knows not what. Here, relief is unlikely until we can find the hidden cause. The same is true of irrational fear of particular things which we know cannot harm us. For example, one man was always afraid of men who wore spectacles, until it was discovered that at four years of age he had been temporarily blinded. This experience had been repressed and forgotten and only after it was brought to consciousness was the irrational fear of men with spectacles got rid of.

Interpreting the expressions of emotions. The expression of the emotions is an important matter for social relationships. Can we judge the depth of a man's emotion by his expression of it ? It is very doubtful. We cannot assume that a mother feels the loss of a child more than the father does because she weeps and he does not. Indeed, a woman herself, the poetess Elizabeth Barrett Browning, has asserted that the profoundest grief is not strongly expressed. She wrote :

"I tell you, hopeless grief is passionless—
That only men incredulous of despair,
Half-taught in anguish through the midnight air,
Beat upward to God's throne in loud access
Of shrieking and reproach. Deep-hearted man, express
Grief for thy Dead in silence like to death."

Think of those who yelled themselves hoarse when they met heroes returning victorious from war. Are they always the ones who now remember them with deepest gratitude and want to see that they are not forgotten ?

Yes, there are often big differences between the depth of emotion and its outward expression. And that itself increases the difficulty of our understanding one another—witness the case of King Lear and Cordelia. Perhaps joy usually betrays itself : grief and depression not always so fully. The suicide of a man through depression has often come as an intense surprise to relatives who never suspected the truth. On the other hand some are accomplished actors and can simulate an emotion, perhaps of affection or of sympathy, that completely deceives others. Here the most useful check is careful observation, for such actors will finally betray themselves in action.

Even when emotion is really felt and strongly expressed, it may be shallow and soon evaporate. Careful observation will show that some people may at one moment express intense emotion, perhaps sympathy, about some bereavement, and the next moment may be showing a lively interest in some local gossip or news in the paper. They are not acting; they simply have shallow emotions, violently expressed but rapidly dying out.*

Misunderstanding the feelings of others. The reader may be wondering how all this about the *expression* of emotions bears on the subject of mental health. The connection lies in the fact that mental health depends to a great extent on satisfactory social relationships, as we have seen in earlier chapters. Now these depend partly on the way we judge one another; and we are very apt to misjudge the inner feelings of others. Careful experiments have shown that even a woman's intuition is not what it has been thought to be; indeed, it is quite as unreliable as that of men.†

* Jane Austen has delightfully depicted a number of women of this type.

† See the present writer's article, "The relative reliability of men and women in intuitive judgements of character," *British Journal of Psychology*, (Volume XIX, 1929).

Because we are so apt to misjudge one another, difficulties may occur between friends, or lovers, between husband and wife, or parents and children. How much were the inner feelings of Elizabeth Browning, the invalid poetress, cooped up in her home, how much were her feelings understood by her tyrant father? And what about that famous family in the country parsonage in Yorkshire which produced those great writers, Charlotte Brontë and her sister Emily? In the apparently placid life of the vicarage did the old vicar ever dream that his daughter Charlotte had the feelings expressed in her novel "Jane Eyre," written in secret, or that Emily as a mere girl was having emotions which led her to write these brave lines:

> "But when the days of golden dreams had perished
> And even Despair was powerless to destroy;
> Then did I learn how existence could be cherished
> Strengthened and fed without the aid of joy."

Many examples could be found of one child in a family who was never understood by the others, and who suffered through that.

Misunderstanding may occur not only through wrong or excessive expressions of feeling, but through repression and failure to express. Think how tongue-tied we often are in expressing out true feelings. I was once told by my mother that her own mother, though she had a fairly happy married life, thought that her husband did not love her deeply because he rarely spoke of it. He was a non-conformist minister, deeply religious and very restrained. There has come into my possession an old diary of his, found after his death, and in one passage he refers to his wife and his deep love for her, and then he adds the words, " Lord save me from idolatry ; " but his wife only read this after his death.

Perhaps I am getting sentimental ; but strange inhibitions can stop the normal expression of feelings, apart from the fact that our British restraint may often be carried too far.

The warping of judgment by emotions. Another important point about emotions is the way they affect our judgement of people and things. We often smile at the lover who thinks his mistress perfect in every way when his friends can see nothing in her : and Shakespeare in one passage even classes the lover and the lunatic together.

The love that is blind devotion may at least sometimes serve a purpose ; but hatred and anger make us equally unbalanced in our judgment of others, and that can do nothing but harm. And further, self interest warps the judgment of men as to social and economic questions, a psychological fact of special importance in a democracy.

Of course, we tend to find good reasons for our prejudices, our loves and hatreds. That is so familiar that psychologists have given it a special label—"rationalization." The man whose pocket will be hard hit by a suggested new tax, readily brings forward reasons why it would be harmful to the economic life of the country: and he may do this quite honestly, unconsciously repressing the real motive behind his attitude. The lover or parent who dotes upon a quite unworthy individual, and who makes some big sacrifice for the loved one, tries to justify it by a defence of the other's conduct which everyone else sees to be extremely flimsy. The same is often true of a man's criticisms of one whom he hates or envies.

In many varied ways we may act from emotion and some hidden impulse and then unwittingly invent reasons for our actions. That such reasons may be quite unconsciously invented will be more readily understood and believed when we consider what may happen under hypnotism and suggestion; illustrations of that will be given in our next chapter.

CHAPTER VI

SUGGESTION, AUTO-SUGGESTION AND THE ATTITUDE TO LIFE

Hypnotism. The best way to understand the working of suggestion is by first considering hypnotism. When a man is hypnotized it is possible to do some remarkable things. First you can tell him that he will feel no pain if you stick a pin in his finger, and if completely hypnotized he will *not* feel it. Second, you may tell him that shortly after you have wakened him he will do some trivial thing—say turn out an electric fire : and on wakening he will soon do so. He will not remember that you told him to do it, and if you ask him why he has done it he will try to give some good reason, perhaps say that it seemed too warm, or that he thought we ought to save electricity in these difficult times. That throws a light on the process of rationalization mentioned at the end of the last chapter, when in ordinary waking life we do an action moved by some unconscious or deep emotional cause, and then try to give some reason for it, quite unaware that we are inventing a reason.

Even without being hypnotized, if a man submits himself for a time willingly to a psychologist he can have it suggested to him that he cannot lift his hand or that he will cease to feel some fear that has oppressed him, and often this suggestion will succeed, at least for a time.*

It may be wondered then why most mental troubles cannot be got rid of through hypnotism. The reason is that the effects are only temporary. Hypnotism is useful chiefly as a means of getting back memories which have been repressed ; but it is at times useful in getting a man to do something, while still under the influence of hypnotic suggestion, which he has declared he cannot do, perhaps going home alone through crowded streets. Then the memory that he has done this and come to no harm, is a help towards further means of cure. For example, one woman who had such a morbid horror of city streets said to me in a bright cheery way just after being wakened from a hypnotic sleep, " I think I'll go and do some shopping." She was quite unaware that during her sleep I had suggested to her that she should go and do some shopping before going home.

In most cases the discovery of the original *cause* of such irrational feelings is necessary : but as we shall see often a great deal can be

* Indeed, even local anaesthesia (insensitiveness) can be produced by suggestion. See *The Neuroses in War*, (page 96) Edited by E. Miller.

done by waking suggestion to change ideas and attitudes which have become fixed in the patient's mind.

The nature of suggestion. Perhaps I should first say what the psychologist means by suggestion. He means the process of getting another person to accept an idea or belief, not by reasoned argument but rather by personal influence and prestige. A great leader carries his supporters with him not only by logical argument but by the force of personality. We are liable to accept the opinions and attitudes of those we feel very superior to us and of those we love.

Now the child is, on the whole, more suggestible than an adult. A young child as a rule tends to accept the beliefs of parents and to adopt their attitudes, especially to matters which are outside his own experience. This is on the whole a useful thing in the stabilization of society. Parental suggestion and example provide the means by which general ideas as to right and wrong are implanted, until the young people are old enough to think and judge for themselves.

Harmful suggestions. But sometimes, harmful ideas or attitudes may remain deeply imbedded in the mind through the powerful early influence of parents. For example, one man of thirty who consulted me said he was in a state of conflict. He wanted to become an engineer, and his experience in the Army had revealed his ability in that direction : but his father wanted him still to remain a clerk. Also, he was greatly attracted by a young woman and thought of marrying her. But his parents had always warned him against marriage and he found it impossible to throw off this influence. It had become less while he was away in the Army, but was returning when he went back home.

In another case I found a marriage being spoiled through the young wife's attitude to sex matters, which she felt to be disgusting. Now, it turned out that her mother had imbued her when she was a girl with these ideas about sex, and the young woman was still dominated by the mother. She was, however, an intelligent young woman, and it was possible, in the first frank talks she had had with anyone about sex matters, to get her to adopt a very different attitude, much to the advantage of the marriage.*

Dr. Hadfield tells of a man who complained of a constant pain in his stomach, which he said he had had from babyhood. It turned

* Dr. Ian Suttie thinks the suggestive influence of the mother is so great that the mother's attitude to the father determines the children's attitude to him. See *The Origins of Love and Hate*, (page 103).

out that once when he had stomach-ache his mother had told him *she* had such a pain some months before he was born and that it was "in the family." The explanation of this influence of suggestion led to the disappearance of the pain.*

Many such examples could be quoted of wrong ideas being implanted and then continuing to produce symptoms by a kind of auto-suggestion. For example, a food which the patient thinks disagrees with him will appear to do so, unless he is unaware that it is an ingredient of what he has eaten. In one case reported by two medical psychologists, a girl who believed that a kiss might lead to pregnancy, began to have abdominal pains which were first diagnosed as due to appendicitis, and only disappeared when the girl's belief was discovered and the true facts explained to her.†

Auto-suggestion. These last cases are examples of a kind of self-suggestion—auto-suggestion as it is called. A great deal of

* See article by J. A. Hadfield in *Functional Nerve Disease*, Edited by Crichton Miller.

† See *Psychological Medicine*, (page 15, 1943) by D. Curran and E. Gutman. The authors report that the girl was actually operated on for appendicitis. Later on the girl was kissed again, and again the abdominal pains returned. Only then were her ideas as to pregnancy discovered.

attention was called to this years ago by the French doctor Coué. He emphasised its importance and claimed that it could bring about remarkable cures, for example by a man constantly suggesting to himself that he was getting well, or more self-confident and so on. The reader may remember that suggested phrase for repeating, "everyday and in everyway I am getting better and better," which became the butt of many a jest.

The vogue of Couéism passed. But we must not merely scoff at the *exaggerated* claims for auto-suggestion. We may admit that at least momentary effects on symptoms can be produced through auto-suggestion. I convinced myself of this many years ago. I happened to be reading Baudouin's book on "*Suggestion and Auto-suggestion*," as I lay in bed with influenza and a very sore throat which hurt acutely when I swallowed. I also had (conveniently for experimental purposes) a poisoned finger which was very tender. I tried auto-suggestion on these, following the recognized procedure and saying to myself, "The pain is going, going," and trying to imagine it gone. I actually succeeded so far that I could press my finger hard without any pain and swallow without discomfort. But alas, the effect was only temporary and back came the pains after a short interval. The effect, however, of auto-suggestion in reference to ***mental attitudes*** may be much more lasting. Unfortunately, the effect may sometimes be bad. Indeed, a man may occasionally do himself harm when he is trying to help himself, just as a man may come to imagine bodily symptoms if he reads a book on diseases. One of my patients had been reading a popular book on psychology and had become convinced, (to a great extent quite wrongly) that he was suffering from various psychological weaknesses. Some people knowing that a grandparent committed suicide or died in a Mental Home, brood over the fact and become convinced that they must do the same. Indeed, the first work of the psychologist is sometimes to break down wrong and harmful ideas fixed in the patient's mind. Then suggestion in the form of interpretation and of persuasion may help towards new ideas and new attitudes.

The right place for suggestion. There is a danger that suggestion alone may deal only with symptoms and not with basic causes: so it may be well to recall here some of the fundamental things discussed in earlier chapters, which may involve essential preliminaries before suggestion can be profitably employed.

First we saw that so-called nervous breakdowns are mainly due to emotional conflict, and that the healthy thing is to *face* the conflict honestly and not to shrink from it or repress it. Then we often have to explore the unconscious if we are to get rid of inferiority or other troublesome complexes, or to eliminate the sources of irritation between people.

We must recall that abnormal loneliness and over sensitiveness may be due to an unconscious mother-complex keeping a grown man at the level of childish needs of mothering; and we saw that such unconscious influences, and perhaps some obscure defence-mechanisms, must be brought to light, even though the process may be at first a painful one.

Even when these matters have been dealt with, however, there is the final need that the conflicting impulses shall be unified by some guiding principle or dominating ideal, and that a new attitude to some aspects of life should be adopted; and in this the influence of the psychologist through suggestion may be paramount.

All this is linked with a wider problem—one which touches the normal individual as well as the neurotic. For everyone the attitude to life is profoundly modified by the influence of others. It may be largely determined by the suggestive influence of parents—or of a great leader. Matthew Arnold found a father and a great leader in one, and so was able to pay a fine tribute to his memory when he wrote :

" And through thee I believe
In the noble and great who are gone ; "

To many the dominant suggestive influence is that of religion, which seeks to produce an attitude through the influence of personality—human or divine, by a faith which transcends reason, a process closely resembling that of suggestion, and not necessarily invalid because of that : for in the realm of experience and especially of mental health, there are some things which become true just because you believe them.

Suggestion and the attitude to life. Perhaps the influence which comes nearest to auto-suggestion is that which we find in reading which we select for the purpose of strengthening in ourselves the ideals we wish to pursue, or to help us to adopt a sounder or braver attitude to life. Indeed, some psychologists have used carefully selected books to encourage in their patients the ideas and attitudes they wish them to adopt.* This method has been used especially with the young ; I still remember that when a boy I was given by my

* See the Chapter on " Biblio-Therapy " in *The Nature and Treatment of Mental Disorders* by Dom Thomas V. Moore, (New York, 1943).

father a book called, "*From Log Cabin to White House,*" and others about the great American leaders. They certainly fired my ambition and admiration. But for adults too, the right literature might be used more extensively for those, not exactly neurotics, who need help in their effort to maintain a calm or cheerful attitude to life.

In such literature reasoned argument has its place. But the appeal of good literature is something more; the beauty of language has its own appeal; and the emotional mood produced by beauty increases suggestibility. A great philosopher once said that if you express an idea clearly, most people would accept it. That was going too far; but an idea expressed clearly *and* beautifully will have a better chance. Even some advertisers, who use suggestion freely, have recognized the value of beauty as an appeal.

Poetry, to those who are sensitive to it, may make the strongest emotional appeal. True it may produce only temporary moods, but many good influences fluctuate in their effects, and our insight into life's meaning and values is not always at its clearest. The mystic is not always seeing visions nor is the Christian always on Mount Pisgah.

We may recall those lines of Wordsworth's, when he refers to:

"That blessed mood
In which the burthern of the mystery,
Of all this unintelligible world,
Is lightened: ———
While with an eye made quiet by the power
Of Harmony, and the deep power of joy,
We see into the life of things."

Wordsworth himself it will be seen, describes this as a "*mood*." But though we rise to such clear vision only at times, the insight may be enough to guide the darker moments. That is the message of those other lines, of Matthew Arnold, with which this chapter may well close.

"We cannot kindle when we will
The fire which in the heart resides;
The Spirit bloweth and is still,
In mystery our soul abides;
But tasks in hours of insight willed
Can be through hours of gloom fulfilled."

CHAPTER VII

CONCLUSION

This little book must of course only be regarded as a brief introduction to a very big subject. In a series of short talks, omissions and limitations are inevitable, but I hope that these few chapters may lead some to a more serious study of the subject, for which a list of books is appended.

It is sometimes said that a little knowledge is a dangerous thing : but, as was pointed out in Chapter I, even the general public are already acquiring a little knowledge, and sometimes a perverted knowledge, of psychological matters. Furthermore, a great deal depends on the attitude towards that "little knowledge." I have tried to produce an attitude of sympathetic openness of mind combined with caution, to stress the fact that minor mental disorders should neither be ignored, nor laughed at, not yet have their importance exaggerated. I have pointed out that a genuine neurosis cannot be got rid of merely by an effort of will, and cannot be helped by the amateur ; though in the case of minor mental troubles and depressions, and of greater troubles for which there are reasonable grounds, a man's attitude to these and to life in general may be helped by some knowledge of psychological facts and through that knowledge, he may gain a better understanding of himself and of others.

I have also mentioned, and would like to stress the importance of ensuring that any possible physical causes have been dealt with by a physician ; though it may be added that a distinguished medical psychologist has protested against the idea that *every* conceivable bodily cause should be dealt with before *any* possible psychological cause is considered.

It will be clear to the reader that physical conditions could not be the cause in many of the examples of minor mental disorders we have given, which could be traced to specific experiences and which then immediately ceased. On the other hand, some physical disorder, even if slight, is often a subsidiary cause. The general reader should also be informed that for some types of neurosis there are various forms of medical treatment, (e.g., drugs or electrotherapy) which are being used but which of course can only, or should only be employed under the direction of a psychiatrist.*

* The medical reader will find these referred to in several of the books given in the list at the end of this Chapter, notably the last four but one in the list.

I have touched at times, but only briefly, on the important question of the relation between the patient and the psychologist. This is not a suitable topic for a short introduction to the subject of psychology and mental health; but psychologists agree that any preliminary dependence on the psychologist should give place eventually to the patient's developing a reliance on himself.

In the general psychology of the unconscious, and in social and moral training, a most important subject is that of sublimation—the deflection of natural impulses on to higher levels consistent with conscience or ideals or the claims of society. This topic has not been discussed here though it is relevant to our problem of the unification of emotional impulses; but I have already treated it at some length elsewhere* and the reader will find ample discussion of it in several of the books I have named in the appended list.

Closely associated with the problem of sublimation is the topic of sex and, with this, Freud's emphasis on the supreme importance of sex in the causation of mental disorders.

* Especially in *The Difficult Child and the Problem of Discipline* and in *The New Psychology of the Unconscious.* The most exhaustive and scholarly treatment of sublimation is given in three articles by Professor J. C. Flugel in *The British Journal of Educational Psychology*, (Volume XII, 1942).

For a study of these subjects the reader should turn to Freud's own writings.* Here, I can only add a few brief statements. First, that practically all who have worked in the field of mental health or have written about it, (e.g., the authors of the books in my list) would readily acknowledge the supreme importance of the work done by Freud as a pioneer in the study of unconscious influences, and of the treatment of mental disorders. Second, most of them would admit the great importance of sex as a source of conflict and repression and the need for our society to face some problems which arise partly from our present social and economic civilisation.

There would also I think, be general agreement that, in a considerable proportion of cases which come before the psychologist, sex

* His *Introductory Lectures* mentioned in my appended list is still, I think, the best of his general books to read first; his later *New Introductory Lectures on Psycho-analysis* being, as he says, rather a continuation of parts of the earlier book, though with some revision of earlier views. Then the reader might turn to some of Freud's ablest exponents—Dr. J. C. Flugel's section on "Psycho-analysis" in an *Outline of Modern Knowledge*, edited by W. Rose, and Dr. Ernest Jones's book given in the list. Then the student should consider some critical examinations of Freud's views about sex which he will find in several of the books in my list (e.g., those by Rivers and McDougall). My own book gives a brief and elementary discussion of the topic.

problems have played some part, interpreting sex here in a wide sense.

On the other hand, most of these representative writers would I think agree that Freud exaggerates the importance of sex in reference to neurosis and pays too little attention to other strong impulses and desires as causes of conflict, and also that Freud is apt to detect sex where it does not exist, especially by the enormous extension of his list of *symbols* of sex appearing in dreams. Alfred Adler, indeed, withdrew from his close association with Freud because of this exaggeration of the place of sex, though Adler himself proceeded to develop his system with an exaggerated emphasis on the importance of self-assertion and the craving for power. (Adler indeed thought that some supposed sexual impulses are really desires for power).

In particular, there is, I think, little evidence for the significance of sex in early childhood to which Feud attached so much importance, a fact which is evident by the now popular use of the term, "Oedipus Complex."*

* I have given a report of an enquiry as to the supposed Oedipus Complex in my *Psychology of Early Childhood*, (Chapter 17 on "Affection for Parents and the Supposed Oedipus Complex") The following Chapter deals with "The Development of Sex and Sex-interests in Infancy." Vigorous criticisms of Feud's views on the Oedipus Complex are given in W. McDougall's *Psycho-analysis and Social Psychology*.

Finally, the eager student should be warned that the psychology of the unconscious and the practical application of psychology to problems of mental health are not easy studies. The first attempts at serious study, beyond introductory works, may well be confusing. Individual writers tend to stress their own special points and those of general agreement are obscured. For a comprehensive understanding, indeed, I should maintain that some knowledge of general psychology is also necessary. Otherwise the abnormal looms too large and explanations of some mental phenomena are apt to be found in subtle and unconscious causes when they might well be explained as general psychological facts of normal and conscious mental experience.

After a lifetime devoted to psychological study, many problems remain obscure and difficult ; but with new evidence slowly accumulating we may hope to come nearer and nearer to such understanding of man as is possible to man himself. To the sceptic on this I would recall that psychology is a relatively new subject which has had to fight a hard battle for recognition as a budding science ; and what might we not have attained by now if one tenth of the amount of money which has been expended in the last century, on say physics and chemistry, had been spent on psychological research? Yet when psychology has done its utmost, not all will have been "explained." The ultimate mystery of man's being must be left for philosophy to wrestle with.

Nor is it only with the more mysterious aspects of the human mind that psychology is concerned. By experiment, observation and statistical analysis, it has built up a great body of knowledge about normal everyday mental processes, which may seem quite ordinary and commonplace processes to the man in the street, but about which his ideas have often proved quite wrong.

The superficial student, indeed, is apt to think that the task of psychologists is mainly to explain what is strange and unusual; for example, why we have weird dreams, or how we can possibly repress and forget stirring emotional experiences. Admittedly that is part of our task, as is implied by much of the contents of this little book. But as my former teacher, James Ward, once said, the great mystery is not why we forget things, but how we come to remember anything; and even prolonged study of psychology should not remove that sense of the wonderful in the apparently simplest of mental processes.

BOOKS FOR FURTHER READING

In the following brief list I have placed the shorter or more readable books first. The later ones are more suitable for medical men or advanced students.

B. Hart	*The Psychology of Insanity*
J. A. Hadfield	*Psychology and Morals*
Crichton Miller	*Psycho-analysis and its Derivatives*
C. W. Valentine	*The New Psychology of the Unconscious*
C. Burt	*The Subnormal Mind* (latter part)
I. D. Suttie	*Origins of Love and Hate*
Crichton Miller (Editor)	*Functional Nerve Disease*
T. A. Ross	*The Common Neuroses*
Marcus Gregory	*Psycho-Therapy, Scientific and Religious*
W. McDougall	*An Outline of Abnormal Psychology*
R. G. Gordon	*The Neurotic Personality*
W. Brown	*Psychological Methods of Healing*
Sigmund Freud	*Introductory Lectures on Psycho-analysis*
Sigmund Freud	*The Psycho-pathology of Everyday Life*
C. Baudouin	*Suggestion and Auto-Suggestion*
Alfred Adler	*The Neurotic Constitution*
Pierre Janet	*Principles of Psycho-Therapy*
Pierre Janet	*Psychological Healing*
W. H. R. Rivers	*Instinct and the Unconscious*
M. Culpin	*Recent Advances in the Study of the Psycho-neuroses*
Ernest Jones	*Papers on Psycho-analysis*
D. Curran and E. Guttman	*Psychological Medicine*
T. V. Moore	*The Nature and Treatment of Mental Disorders* (New York)
E. Miller (Editor)	*The Neuroses in War*
D. K. Henderson and R. D. Gillespie	*Text-book of Psychiatry*
R. Gordon (Editor)	*A Survey of Child Psychiatry*

INDEX

INDEX

PRINTED BY THE THANET PRESS,
UNION CRESCENT, MARGATE, KENT

For Product Safety Concerns and Information please contact our EU
representative GPSR@taylorandfrancis.com
Taylor & Francis Verlag GmbH, Kaufingerstraße 24, 80331 München, Germany

www.ingramcontent.com/pod-product-compliance
Ingram Content Group UK Ltd.
Pitfield, Milton Keynes, MK11 3LW, UK
UKHW022158190926
475702UK00003B/90

* 9 7 8 1 1 3 8 8 9 9 6 3 6 *